Blues and Bliss
The Poetry of George Elliott Clarke

Blues and Bliss
The Poetry of George Elliott Clarke

Selected
with an
introduction by
Jon Paul Fiorentino
and an
afterword by
George Elliott Clarke

lps
LAURIER POETRY SERIES

Wilfrid Laurier University Press

WLU

We acknowledge the support of the Canada Council for the Arts for our publishing program. We acknowledge the financial support of the Government of Canada through the Book Publishing Industry Development Program for our publishing activities.

 Canada Council
for the Arts

Conseil des Arts
du Canada

 ONTARIO ARTS COUNCIL
CONSEIL DES ARTS DE L'ONTARIO

Library and Archives Canada Cataloguing in Publication

Clarke, George Elliott, 1960–
      Blues and bliss : the poetry of George Elliott Clarke / selected with
an introduction by Jon Paul Fiorentino ; and an afterword by George Elliott Clarke.

(Laurier poetry series)
ISBN 978-1-55458-060-6

  I. Fiorentino, Jon Paul   II. Title.   III. Series.

PS8555.L3748B59 2008   C811'.54   C2008-905842-9

© 2008 Wilfrid Laurier University Press
Waterloo, Ontario, Canada N2L 3C5
www.wlupress.wlu.ca

The front cover reproduces a painting titled *Ramble* (ca. 1953), by William L. Clarke (1935–2005). Cover and text design by P.J. Woodland.

Every reasonable effort has been made to acquire permission for copyright material used in this text, and to acknowledge all such indebtedness accurately. Any errors and omissions called to the publisher's attention will be corrected in future printings.

♾

This book is printed on Ancient Forest Friendly paper (100% post-consumer recycled).

Printed in Canada

Table of Contents

Foreword

At the beginning of the twenty-first century, poetry in Canada—writing and publishing it, reading and thinking about it—finds itself in a strangely conflicted place. We have many strong poets continuing to produce exciting new work, and there is still a small audience for poetry; but increasingly, poetry is becoming a vulnerable art, for reasons that don't need to be rehearsed.

But there are things to be done: we need more real engagement with our poets. There needs to be more access to their work in more venues—in classrooms, in the public arena, in the media—and there needs to be more, and more different kinds, of publications that make the wide range of our contemporary poetry more widely available.

The hope that animates this series from Wilfrid Laurier University Press is that these volumes help to create and sustain the larger readership that contemporary Canadian poetry so richly deserves. Like our fiction writers, our poets are much celebrated abroad; they should just as properly be better known at home.

Our idea is to ask a critic (sometimes herself a poet) to select thirty-five poems from across a poet's career; write an engaging, accessible introduction; and have the poet write an afterword. In this way, we think that the usual practice of teaching a poet through eight or twelve poems from an anthology is much improved upon; and readers in and out of classrooms will have more useful, engaging, and comprehensive introductions to a poet's work. Readers might also come to see more readily, we hope, the connections among, as well as the distances between, the life and the work.

It was the ending of an Al Purdy poem that gave Margaret Laurence the epigraph for *The Diviners*: "but they had their being once/and left a place to stand on." Our poets still do, and they are leaving many places to stand on. We hope that this series helps, variously, to show how and why this is so.

—*Neil Besner*
General Editor

Biographical Note

Born in Windsor, Nova Scotia, in 1960, George Elliott Clarke is the son of William and Geraldine Clarke, descendants of African American, Cree, and Barbadian immigrants to Nova Scotia. Raised in Halifax, Nova Scotia, in North End working-class, immigrant, multicultural, and military neighbourhoods, Clarke attended Alexandra, Joseph Howe, and Bloomfield schools, and then Queen Elizabeth High School. As a student at the University of Waterloo, 1979–84, he earned an Honours B.A. in English. At Dalhousie University, 1986–89, he took an M.A. in English, and at Queen's University, 1990–93, Clarke garnered a Ph.D. in English. Before commencing his academic career, he worked as a tutor (1979), library programmer (1980), office clerk (1981), Ontario legislative researcher (1982–83), newspaper editor (1984–85, 1986–87), social worker (1985–86), parliamentary aide (1987–91), newspaper columnist (1988–89, 1992–present), and freelance writer and screenwriter (1991–93). In 1994, Clarke was appointed assistant professor of English and Canadian Studies at Duke University. He also served as the Seagram Visiting Chair in Canadian Studies at McGill University (1998–99). In 1999, Clarke accepted an appointment at the University of Toronto, where he is the inaugural E.J. Pratt Professor of Canadian Literature, a position established specifically for a poet-professor.

In the quarter-century since his first book appeared, Clarke has issue nine poetry texts (including this one), three chapbooks, four plays in verse (and three opera libretti), a novel, a scholarly essay collection, and edited two anthologies. His plays and operas (one composed by James Rolfe and two composed by D.D. Jackson) have all been staged, and his two screenplays have been televised. He has two titles in translation, one in Chinese and another in Romanian. He lives in Toronto but still owns property in Nova Scotia, near Windsor.

Acclaimed for his poetry, opera libretti, and novel, Clarke has also won laurels for his work as an anthologist and scholar of African Canadian literature, a field of study that he has pioneered. His honours include the Archibald Lampman Award for Poetry (1991), the Portia White Prize for Artistic Excellence (1998), a Bellagio Center (Italy) Fellowship (1998), the Governor-General's Literary Award for Poetry (2001), the National Magazine Gold Award for Poetry (2001), the Dr. Martin Luther King, Jr. Achievement

Award (2004), the Pierre Elliott Trudeau Fellowship Prize (2005), the Frontieras Poesis Premiul (Romania, 2005), the Estelle and Ludwig Jus Memorial Human Rights Award (2005), the Dartmouth Book Award for Fiction (2006), Appointment to the Order of Nova Scotia (2006), and Appointment to the Order of Canada (2008). Clarke has also received five honorary doctorates.

Introduction

Blues and Bliss: Negotiating the Polyphony of George Elliott Clarke

The blues singer, the preacher, the cultural critic, the exile, the Africadian, the high modernist, the spoken word artist; the Canadian poet. These are some of the voices and identities of George Elliott Clarke. His influences are many. Derek Walcott, Amiri Baraka, Ezra Pound, Wallace Stevens, and many others are intertextually linked to his practice. He is a poet who seems at times haunted by the anxiety of influence, but a closer reading of his texts reveals that the multiple voices of George Elliott Clarke are the result of his poetic fluency and scholarly acuity.

Clarke's poetics negotiate cultural space through adherence to and revision of tradition. A collection like *Whylah Falls* establishes a voice for the Africadian community—a voice that employs diverse poetic strategies such as iambic pentameter, the Mississippi Delta blues, and modernist *vers libre*. A collection like *Blue* establishes equally multivocal poetic voices, but its various strategies are deployed to a more polemical/performative end.

Some of Clarke's many voices and influences can be seen by looking at the following excerpt from Derek Walcott's poem "Homecoming: Anse La Raye":

> sugar-headed children race
> pelting up from the shallows
> because your clothes,
> your posture
> seem a tourist's.
> They swarm like flies
> round your heart's sore.
>
> Suffer them to come,
> entering their needle's eye
> knowing whether they live or die,
> what others make of life will pass them by
> like that far silvery freighter
> threading the horizon like a toy;

for once, like them,
you wanted no career
but this sheer light, this clear,
infinite, boring, paradisal sea,
but hoped it would mean something to declare
today, I am your poet, yours,
all this you knew,
but never guessed you'd come
to know there are homecomings without home.

You give them nothing.

The crisis of exile illustrated by Walcott in the above excerpt was one faced by Clarke after a disastrous reading in front of his community. After this formative experience, Clarke swore that he would never write poetry that was inaccessible to his community.

Clarke was reading poems from his first collection, *Saltwater Spirituals*, when he was heckled mercilessly: "So people started yelling at me: 'Get off the stage.' It was very direct: 'You're boring. Go home.' The people didn't want to hear some dry shit" (Compton, 145). He discovered that his poems from that collection could not be performed in a way that spoke to his community. His solution to this disconnect is found in the polyphony of his more recent work, from *Whylah Falls* to *Black*: these are poems that combine abstract, intellectual, and specific literary content with a home-place vernacular. These poems are meant to be sung as well as to thrive on the page. (Although I am using the term "polyphony" to denote multivocal verse, the musical connotations of the term can be applied to Clarke's texts as well.) The poem "The Symposium" includes the following imperative: "sit back, relax and be black" (stanza 1). As Clarke has grown as a poet and intellectual, he has simultaneously adhered to his own advice.

The influence of Walcott, the "Commonwealth Bard," on Clarke is based on more than just one biographical intersection. Formally, both poets strive for a hyper-literate, high modernism. Clarke looks to Walcott's "blackening of English" as a movement out of exile. In fact, the notion of exile-as-trope is the essential point of departure for both writers. Consider this excerpt from Clarke's open letter to Walcott: "I write in a cold place where I possess beleaguered rights. Canada wants nothing to do with any combustible sorrow or inflammatory blues. It demands a clipped, precise speech, some tone of majesty to restrict American slovenliness, republican vulgarity. It demands metre akin to its own War Measures Act. The climate will hardly let you spark any fire. But your books are portable infernos I use to warm and illuminate this hostile, killing environment. I write to you and I have no right. Commonwealth Bard, born thirty years before I was born, born in another backwater province (but warmer than where I was born), born in an era of war, I thank you for pioneering a way of blackening English, of roasting syllables upon the righteous fires of your anger and your love until they split and crack. You cannibalize the Canon and invite your brethren and sistren to the intoxicating, exhilarating feast" (16–17). It is interesting to note that Derek Walcott wrote much of his celebrated verse in New England—a climate that is not altogether disparate from Clarke's Nova Scotia.

Both Clarke and Walcott want to engage the canon, and both mythologize "non-literary territory" (i.e., St. Lucia for Walcott, Nova Scotia for Clarke)— and both poets share the Atlantic. And, as noted, both poets desire the poetics of exile—the negotiation/renegotiation of the community from the position of the exile (in the case of Walcott and Clarke, the exile is self-determined) and the inevitable revision of the community to integrate a new poetics or worldview. Clarke's evocation of Walcott as Commonwealth Bard illustrates that this is a post-colonial modality as much as it is specifically a Canadian one. The essential difference in the two poets' respective points of departure lies in the distinction between the Caribbean colonial experience and the African American/Africadian experience.

The poem "Look Homeward, Exile" (page 8) is a suitable example of both Clarke's fixation on the Walcottesque and his fixation on the tropes of home and exile. The nostalgic voice is X's: "I can still see that soil crimsoned by butchered / Hog and imbrued with rye, lye, and homely / Spirituals everybody must know" (lines 1–3). The crimsoned soil foreshadows the death of Othello Clemence. Besides the spilled blood, the earth is also marked with rye, lye, and spirituals. The imagistic establishment of the home place occurs at once within the first few lines of X's reminiscences. From this position of retrospect, the exiled poet cannot be soothed: "Still, nothing warms my wintry exile—neither / Prayers nor fine love, neither votes nor hard drink" (lines 30–31). Despite the familiar iambic lines and the seemingly cathartic subject matter of nostalgic memory, the poet remains outside of home. The exiled X provides us with a more than sufficient hook for the sweeping, extravagant narrative-based poem sequence that follows.

Anne Compton makes the following observation regarding *Whylah Falls* and geography/history: "*Whylah Falls* mythologizes a specific place (Weymouth Falls, N.S.) and an event (the killing of Graham Cromwell), but it does even more than that. Under the pressure of events (the razing of Africville and Cromwell's death), it reconceptualizes a people and a 200-year-old history in mythic terms" (139). In other words, Weymouth Falls is the historical/geographical home place; Whylah Falls is its fictional/mythic analogue. The Sissiboo is the historical/geographical home place; Sixhiboux River is the fictional/mythic analogue; Cromwell's death is the historical/sociological event; Othello Clemence's death is the fictional/mythic analogue.

Despite efforts to establish a poetic voice of the Africadian community, Clarke, like Walcott, cannot resist a corresponding and consistent fetishization of "Literature in English" (i.e., "Albion"), from the classical to romanticism to high modernism. Shakespeare, Shelley, Milton, Chaucer, Eliot, Yeats, etc., are consistently evoked. Is this an effort to legitimize the text? To include the Hegelian master–slave binary within Africadian poetics (like Walcott)? To acknowledge the prosodic and thematic literary modalities that Clarke cannot seem to live without? *Saltwater Spirituals* was written entirely in free verse. Clarke confesses that he was never at home within this tradition: "I've never been comfortable within unfettered free verse even though I was writing it in *Saltwater Spirituals*. I needed blank verse.... This is the way we speak" (Compton, 147). The notion that there is something natural about the iambic pentameter, that it is the closest textual, poetic transcription to the speech patterns of English, seems archaic. Perhaps Clarke meant to say "this is the way we sing." Clarke goes on to uncover a much more compelling reason for the persistence of the sonnet, and of blank verse in Canadian poetry, saying: "I think this [the sonnet form] is also postcolonial. We have inherited this thing. Now what can we do with it?" (Compton, 148).

What appears clear to me is that the communal poetic voice is sometimes too ironically informed by Clarke's hyper-literate and colonial training in literature. The attempt at negotiation of inherited language seems clear, but I cannot help but think back on the community response to *Saltwater Spirituals* and wonder if Clarke always manages to reach the community he desires.

There is a caution in Clarke's 2000 collection, *Blue*. Clarke's poetic voice warns, "No child should read me! / Some lines are encased in ice (chiefly the ones inked for a slut)" (136). This ironic utterance refers to the anticipated resistance of readers to embrace the poetic voice's indulgence. Clarke indulges in poetic practice as far-reaching as performative rhetoric and as conventional as the traditional Eurocentric, Petrarchan sonnet in this text. Inspired by poets ranging from Ovid to Ezra Pound to Amiri Baraka, Clarke succeeds in conjuring up a plurality of poetic voices that range from imagistic to politically stunning to appalling. The polyphonic success of *Blue* is based on its ability to perform poetic difference (i.e., the ability to perform the difference between the self and other, the subject and object) within the subjectivity of one poetic voice. (There is a quite different realization of polyphony in *Whylah Falls*.) In the section of *Blue* entitled *Black Eclogues*,

Clarke manages to evoke the most strategic elements of vitriol in his homage to Baraka's aesthetic in the poem entitled "Calculated Offensive" (page 34). Here, the poetic voice rages:

> To hell with Pound!
> What we desire is African:
> Europe is so septic: it seeps poisons. (lines 1–3)
>
> . . . .
>
> Put Europe to the torch:
> All of Michelangelo's dripping, syphilitic saints,
> all of Sappho's insipid, anorexic virgins. (lines 15–17)

Compare Clarke's rage against Eurocentrism with Baraka's original incendiary text entitled "Black Art" (Baraka, 998):

> We want "poems that kill."
> Assassin poems, Poems that shoot
> guns. Poems that wrestle cops into alleys
> and take their weapons leaving them dead
> with tongues pulled out and sent back to Ireland.

Note that both Baraka and Clarke employ the collective "we" as a rhetorical device, drawing in or excluding the reader, depending on his/her ethnicity. What is achieved in this brief, emulative poem is the revelation of hyperbolic language: how it succeeds in evoking emotion, anger, or discussion in both Clarke's text and in Baraka's. The skilfully written rhetoric reminds me that poetic language needs to function in a hyperbolic mode. Whether the aim is the image or the idea, modes of rhetoric and/or figurative language are dependent on hyperbole. This is the essential truth that poets like Baraka teach us.

What is at stake in any text such as Clarke's *Blue* is whether the poet has the ability to persuade his/her reader into his/her performative realm. What emerges here is a lyric "I" that replaces the rhetorical "we" in poems that pine for, and spit on, Pound, Yeats, et al.:

> Imbibing libretti and bleak liqueur,
> I dread the dim shade of dour, spectral Yeats—
>
> and defrocked, unsavoury Pound, who liked
> to put "negroes" in lower-case (in their place). (lines 1–4)
>
> . . . .
>
> your voice your own (Auden in the margins,
> Eliot, Yeats, and Pound in the dungeon),
>
> a veriloquous, unadulterated voice,
> extracting black blues from a yellowed Oxford. (lines 23–26)

The title of the poem from which the above text is quoted is "Onerous Canon" (page 38). The notion of canon reformation and/or canon revision is an ever-present preoccupation of Clarke's.

In a poem from *Blue* entitled "I. i" (page 41), an anaphoric and powerful piece is found that defines Clarke's notion of "blue" within the context of plurality and complexity: "Blue is a noose strangling the vulnerable sky / Blue is a generic nigger, a genre nigger, an angry nigger / … Blue is a guitar in a Wallace Stevens sonnet carved from *The Cenci* / … Blue is Hitler in bed with Chamberlain in Munich with Eva Braun" (lines 1–8).

The notion of "blue" is about the African Canadian experience (as opposed to Africadian in *Whylah Falls*). However, the text attempts to transcend ethnicity and performs complex, perverse juxtapositions: Stevens's triumphant "The Man with the Blue Guitar" is referenced here, alongside the image of the "genre nigger, … angry nigger." What Clarke captures is the weight of poetic history: the historical presence (Stevens's canonical text) and the historical absence (Clarke's genre/angry nigger). Aside from the specific poems that are elegies, the entire text can be read as elegiac longing for an African Canadian/Acadian history and mourning of the history that has been lost or put under erasure.

Critic Judith Butler insists on the importance of "troubling" language, of making "troubling" an active verb. Butler is referring to processes of performative language: rhetoric, hyperbole, energetic language (and I would add polyphonic language) that bears witness to, and engages in, itself and the other. Clarke's unapologetic engagement of literary/poetic tradition, his use of polyphony and hybridity, and his preoccupation with the negotiation and renegotiation of cultural imperatives, is both effective and troubling. This is language that doesn't just rest on the page. Clarke's astounding poetic skill and attention to detail allow him to engage in the process of "troubling" where a lesser poet would certainly falter. In fact, it is important to note that Clarke's most recent collection at the time of this writing, *Black*, is a further extension of his project of eloquent "troubling." And *Black* contains some of Clarke's finest work to date.

In a seminal moment, Clarke reveals near the end of *Blue* that his poetic voice is concerned with the notion of content and intent: "Is it grace?" Throughout his oeuvre, Clarke achieves great heights through polyphony that coheres—an impressive and compelling blend of blues and bliss.

—*Jon Paul Fiorentino*

Some of the text above is adapted from an earlier essay, "Blackening English: The Polyphonic Poetics of George Elliott Clarke." The footnotes on page 10 and 36 are Clarke's own.

Bibliography

Baraka, Amiri. "Black Art." *The Norton Anthology of African American Literature.*
  New York: W.W. Norton, 1997.
Butler, Judith. *Gender Trouble.* New York: Routledge, 1990.
Clarke, George Elliott. *Blue.* Vancouver: Polestar, 2000.
————. "George Elliott Clarke to Derek Walcott." *Open Letter* 11, no. 3 (Fall 2001).
————. *Whylah Falls.* Vancouver: Polestar, 2000.
Compton, Anne. "Standing Your Ground: George Elliott Clarke in Conversation."
  Studies in Canadian Literature 23, no. 2 (1998).
Walcott, Derek. *Selected Poetry.* London: Heinemann, 1981.

Salvation Army Blues

Seeking after hard things —
muscular work or sweat-swagger action —
I rip wispy, Help Wanted ads,
dream of water-coloured sailors
pulling apart insect wings of maps,
stagger down saxophone blues avenues
where blackbirds cry for crumbs.
I yearn to be Ulyssean, to roam
foaming oceans or wrest
a wage from tough, mad adventure.

For now, I labour language,
earn a cigarette
for a poem, a coffee
for a straight answer,
and stumble, punch-drunk,
down these drawn-and-quartered streets,
tense hands manacled
to snarling pockets.

Halifax Blues

Junked cars bunch, hunch like rats; laundry,
Lynched, dangles from clotheslines; streetlamps sputter,
Gutter, blow out; gross, bloated cops
Awake and pummel Lysol-scented drunks,
While God grins at scabbed girls who scour the streets
To pass pestilence to legislators.
    The harbour crimps like a bent, black cripple;
It limps, drops dead on rocks: each wave's a crutch
That's pitilessly kicked aside. Above,
Grim gulls beats nights with wings that beat back rain.
    I drag poems from the water's muffled black.
They chomp, wriggle, and thrash on *Love's* bloody,
Two-pronged hook. I slap them, writhing still,
On paper, and cry beautiful darkness —
The baroque scream of a feeling. Hurt crows
Caw my sorrow better than a thousand white
Doves. I skulk beneath fainting streetlamps
To disturb taverns, set cops ill at ease.

Hammonds Plains African Baptist Church

      Drunk with light,
I remember maritime country.
I cry Birchtown blues, the stark,
sad beauty of this Kimmerian land.
      I dream of a faithful dory
battling the blue, cruel combers
of a feral, runaway ocean —
a Trotskyite ocean in permanent revolution —
turning fluid ideas over and over
in its leviathan mind,
turning driftwood, drums, and conundrums
over and over....
      Then, crazy with righteous anger,
I think of Lydia Jackson,
slave madonna, soon rich with child,
whose Nova Scotian owner,
the distinguished Dr. Bulman,
kicked her hard in the stomach,
struck her viciously with fire tongs,
and then went out upon the ocean
in his dory
to commune with God.

Campbell Road Church

       At Negro Point, some forgot sleep
to spy the fire-and-brimstone sun
blaze all gold-glory
over a turquoise harbour
of half-sunken, rusted ships,
when it was easy to worship
Benin bronze dawns,
to call "hosanna" to archangel gulls....
But none do now.
       Rather, an ancient CN porter lusts
for Africville —
beautiful Canaan of stained glass and faith,
now limbo of shattered glass and promises,
rats rustling like a mayor's robe.
       He rages to recall
the gutting death of his genealogy,
to protest his home's slaughter
by homicidal bulldozers
and city planners molesting statistics.
       At Negro Point, some forgot sleep,
wailed, "Oh freedom over me,"
heard mournful trains cry like blizzards
along blue Bedford Basin....
       None do now.

Watercolour for Negro Expatriates in France

What are calendars to you?
And, indeed, what are atlases?
　　Time is cool jazz in Bretagne,
You, hidden in berets or eccentric scarves,
somewhere over the rainbow —
where you are tin-men requiring hearts,
lion-men demanding courage,
scarecrow-men needing minds all your own
after DuBois made blackness respectable.
　　Geography is brown girls in Paris
in the spring by the restless Seine
flowing like blood in chic, African colonies;
Josephine Baker on your bebop phonographs
in the lonely, brave, old rented rooms;
Gallic wines shocking you out of yourselves,
leaving you as abandoned
as obsolete locomotives whimpering Leadbelly blues
in lonesome Shantytown, U.S.A.

　　What are borders/frontiers to you?
In actual seven-league sandals,
you ride Monet's shimmering waterlilies —
in your street-artist imaginations —
across the sky darkened,
here and there, by Nazi shadows,
Krupp thunderclouds,
and, in other places, by Americans
who remind you
that you are niggers,
even if you have read Victor Hugo.
　　Night is winged Ethiopia in the distance,
rising on zeta beams of radio free Europe,
bringing you in for touchdown at Orleans;
or, it is strange, strychnine streetwalkers,

fleecing you for an authentic Negro poem
or rhythm and blues salutation.
This is your life —
lounging with Richard White in Matisse-green
parks, facing nightmares of contorted
lynchers every night. Every night.

Scatological ragtime reggae haunts the caverns
of *le métro*. You pick up English-language
newspapers and *TIME* magazines,
learn that this one was arrested,
that one assassinated;
fear waking — like Gregor Samsa —
in the hands of a mob;
lust for a black Constance Chatterley,
not even knowing that
all Black people not residing in Africa
are kidnap victims.
After all, how can you be an expatriate
of a country that was
never yours?

Pastel paintings on Paris pavement,
wall-posters Beardsley-styled:
you pause and admire them all;
and France entrances you
with its kaleidoscope cafés,
chain-smoking intelligentsia,
absinthe and pernod poets....
Have you ever seen postcards
of Alabama or Auschwitz,
Mussolini or Mississippi?
It is unsafe to wallow in Ulyssean dreams,
genetic theories, vignettes of Gertrude Stein,
Hemingway, other maudlin moderns,
while the godless globe

detonates its war-heart, loosing
goose-stepping geniuses
and dark, secret labs.

        Perhaps I suffer aphasia.
I know not how to talk to you.
I send you greeting from *Afrique*
and spirituals of catholic *Négritude*
        Meanwhile, roses burst like red stars,
a flower explodes for a special sister.
You do not accept gravity in France
where everything floats on the premise
that the earth will rise to meet it
the next day;
where the Eiffel Tower bends over backwards
to insult the Statue of Liberty;
and a woman in the flesh of the moment
sprouts rainbow butterfly wings
and kisses a schizoid sculptor
lightly on his full, ruby lips;
and an argument is dropped over cocoa
by manic mulatto musicians
who hear whispers of Eliot —
or Ellington —
in common prayers.

        You have heard Ma Rainey, Bessie Smith.
You need no passports.
Your ticket is an all-night room
facing the ivory, voodoo moon,
full of Henri Rousseau lions and natives;
and your senses, inexplicably
homing in on gorgeous Ethiopia,
while Roman rumours of war
fly you home.

Look Homeward, Exile

I can still see that soil crimsoned by butchered
Hog and imbrued with rye, lye, and homely
Spirituals everybody must know,
Still dream of folks who broke or cracked like shale:
Pushkin, who twisted his hands in boxing,
Marrocco, who ran girls like dogs and got stabbed,
Lavinia, her teeth decayed to black stumps,
Her lovemaking still in demand, spitting
Black phlegm — her pension after twenty towns,
And Toof, suckled on anger that no Baptist
Church could contain, who let wrinkled Eely
Seed her moist womb when she was just thirteen.
   And the tyrant sun that reared from barbed-wire
Spewed flame that charred the idiot crops
To Depression, and hurt my granddaddy
To bottle after bottle of sweet death,
His dreams beaten to one, tremendous pulp,
Until his heart seized, choked; his love gave out.
   But Beauty survived, secreted
In freight trains snorting in their pens, in babes
Whose faces were coal-black mirrors, in strange
Strummers who plucked Ghanaian banjos, hummed
Blind blues — precise, ornate, rich needlepoint,
In sermons scorched with sulphur and brimstone,
And in my love's dark, orient skin that smelled
Like orange peels and tasted like rum, good God!
   I remember my Creator in the old ways:
I sit in taverns and stare at my fists;
I knead earth into bread, spell water into wine.
Still, nothing warms my wintry exile — neither
Prayers nor fine love, neither votes nor hard drink:
For nothing heals those saints felled in green beds,
Whose loves are smashed by just one word or glance
Or pain — a screw jammed in thick, straining wood.

The Wisdom of Shelley

You come down, after
five winters, X,
bristlin' with roses
and words words words,
brazen as brass.
Like a late blizzard,
You bust in our door,
talkin' April and snow and rain,
litterin' the table
with poems —
as if we could trust them!

I can't.
I heard pa tell ma
how much and much he
loved loved loved her
and I saw his fist
fall so gracefully
against her cheek,
she swooned.

Roses
got thorns.
And words
do lie.

I've seen love
die.

The River Pilgrim: A Letter[1]

At eighteen, I thought the Sixhiboux wept.
Five years younger, you were lush, beautiful
Mystery; your limbs — scrolls of deep water.
Before your home, lost in roses, I swooned,
Drunken in the village of Whylah Falls,
And brought you apple blossoms you refused,
Wanting Hank Snow woodsmoke blues and dried smelts,
Wanting some milljerk's dumb, unlettered love.

That May, freights chimed xylophone tracks that rang
To Montréal. I scribbled postcard odes,
Painted *le fleuve Saint-Laurent comme la Seine* —
Sad watercolours for Negro exiles
In France, and dreamt Paris white with lepers,
Soft cripples who finger pawns under elms,
Drink blurry into young debauchery,
Their glasses clear with Cointreau, rain, and tears.

You hung the moon backwards, crooned crooked poems
That no voice could straighten, not even O
Who stroked guitars because he was going
To die with a bullet through his stomach.
Innocent, you curled among notes — petals
That scaled glissando from windows agape,
And remained in southwest Nova Scotia,
While I drifted, sad and tired, in the east.

I have been gone four springs. This April, pale
Apple blossoms blizzard. The garden flutes
E-flats of lilacs, G-sharps of lilies.
Too many years, too many years, are past....

---

[1] This poem is a deliberate revisiting of American poet Ezra Pound's 1915 lyric titled,
"The River Merchant's Wife: A letter," itself a translation of Chinese poet Li Po's
poem, "Song of Chang-Kan."

Past the marble and pale flowers of Paris,
Past the broken, Cubist guitars of Arles,
Shelley, I am coming down through the narrows
Of the Sixhiboux River. I will write
Beforehand. Please, please come out to meet me
                    As far as Gilbert's Cove.

Blank Sonnet

The air smells of rhubarb, occasional
Roses, or first birth of blossoms, a fresh,
Undulant hurt, so body snaps and curls
Like flower. I step through snow as thin as script,
Watch white stars spin dizzy as drunks, and yearn
To sleep beneath a patchwork quilt of rum.
I want the slow, sure collapse of language
Washed out by alcohol. Lovely Shelley,
I have no use for measured, cadenced verse
If you won't read. Icarus-like, I'll fall
Against this page of snow, tumble blackly
Across vision to drown in the white sea
That closes every poem — the white reverse
That cancels the blackness of each image.

The Symposium

Don't gimme nothin' to jaw about, Missy, and I won't have nothin'
to holler for! Just sit back, relax, and be black. I'm gonna learn you
'bout the mens so you can 'scape the bitter foolishness I've suffered. A
little thoughtful can save you trouble.

Missy, you gotta lie to get a good man. And after you gets him, you
gotta be set to hurt him to hold him, so help my Chucky! 'Cos if you
don't or won't or can't, you're gonna be stepped on, pushed 'round,
walked out on, beat up on, cheated on, worked like a black fool, and
cast out your own house.

Don't suck your teeth and cut your eyes at me! I be finished in a
hot second. But you'll hear this gospel truth so long you, my oldest, eat
and sleep in my house. Best cut your sass!

Pack a spare suitcase, one for him. If he proves devilish, it be easier
to toss him out that way. Put one change of clothes into it so he can't
beg and bug you for nothin'!

If he be too quiet, he'll ruminate and feel that bottle more than he
will you. Rum'll be his milk and meat for months. It'll spoil him for
anything. Won't be fit to drive his nail no mo'. So when he's sleepy
drunk, smack the long-ass son of a gun in the head, tell him to wake
his black-ass body up, and drive him out. If the fair fool don't come
back sober, he don't come back. Am I lyin'?

And if he be sweet-lookin', a heavy-natured man, always pullin' on
women, and he takes up with some spinny bitch all daddlied up
from the cash he's vowed to bring you, just tell him right up and down
that you ain't his monkey in a dress, and raise particular devil. Don't
give him no shakes. And if that don't work, don't waste another black
word, grab yourself a second man.

Watch out for two-faced chroniclers. These women will grin in your face, lookin' for news 'bout you and your man. And just when you trust their trashy talk and make your man groan and grump and get all upset, these gold-dust whores creep behind your back, crawl right in your bed, and thief him away. That's how they act. I know: I've been gypped so bloody much. And they don't care if it's a used love, a second-hand love, a stolen love, 'cos it's love all the same. And if it's good to you, they'll try to trick some too. So don't put no business on the streets that's conducted 'tween your sheets. But if some big-mouth humbugs you, tell the black bitch not to mess 'cos she's terrible lookin' anyway; a knife gash 'cross her face would just be improvement.

Missy! Gimme some of that bottle! Preachin' parches the throat. Besides, my eyes feel kinda zigzaggy today.

If some bitch is grinnin' at your man, tell her straight: "If it was shit that I had, you'd want some of that too." Make her skedaddle. If her fresh fool follows, take everything he got and don't give a single, black penny back!

Missy, life's nothin' but guts, muscle, nerve. All you gotta do is stay black and die.

Rose Vinegar

In his indefatigable delirium of love, Xavier wires rugosa rose
blossoms to Shelley. Deluded by his quixotic romanticism, he cannot
yet appreciate the practical necessities of friendship. But, Shelley trusts
in reason; thus, though she admires the blossoms for their truthfulness
to themselves, she does not hesitate to distill a delicate and immortal
vinegar from what she considers the ephemeral petals of X's desire. An
ornament becomes an investment. She fills a cup with the fresh rose
petals; then, stripping off their heels, (the white part), she pours the
petals into a quart sealer and adds two cups of white vinegar. Then, she
seals the jar and places it on the sunny livingroom windowsill for
sixteen days, seven hours, and nine minutes. When the vinegar is
ready, she strains it through a sieve and then pours it back into the
bottle.

Rose vinegar. It's especially good on salads.

Blues for X

Pretty boy, towel your tears,
And robe yourself in black.
Pretty boy, dry your tears,
You know I'm comin' back.
I'm your lavish lover
And I'm slavish in the sack.

Call me Sweet Potato,
Sweet Pea, or Sweety Pie,
There's sugar on my lips
And honey in my thighs.
Jos'phine Baker bakes beans,
But I stew pigtails in rye.

My bones are guitar strings
And blues the chords you strum.
My bones are slender flutes
And blues the bars you hum.
You wanna stay my man,
Serve me whisky when I come.

Vision of Justice

I see the moon hunted down, spooked from hills,
Roses hammer his coffin shut, O stilled
By stuttered slander, judicial gossip,
And a killer's brawling bullet. Bludgeoned
Men, noosed by loose law, swing from pines; judges,
Chalked commandants, gabble dour commandments;
Their law books yawn like lime-white, open pits
Lettered with bones, charred gibberish, of those
Who dared to love or sing and fell to mobs.
Language has become volatile liquor,
Firewater, that lovers pour for prophets
Whom haul, from air, tongues of pentecostal fire —
Poetry come among us.

Chancy's Menu

Taste Grand Pré wine,
Annapolis sharp cheese,
Windsor salt butter,
Madeira Portuguese;
Jamaican dark rum,
Adam's rain-pale ale,
Pickled melon, chicken,
Cornbread, spiced pigtails;
Oysters, fried scallops,
Gaspereaux, and clams,
Queen Eliza cake,
Apples, sides-a-ham;
Sour coffee, sweet cream,
And chokecherry pie,
A wicked kick of whisky,
Newfie screech, or rye.

Chancy's Drinking Song

Make those fiddles quarrel,
Fideles, like gulls, now that daylight's down
And my daughter's come,
Then break out
Steps that stamp like rain
Smashing on a window, sing
With voices that sound like wine
Pissing from a fat stomach,
Or like the brook,
Breathing like a Romeo;
Jupe and swing and whoop!

Beatrice's Defence

My life's a prison that *Death* will unlock.
Like Marie-Josèphe Angélique,
Like Évangéline Bellefontaine,
I'll suffer what I must.

There'll be no blossom on the branch, no tides washing the
face or breast, no salvific kiss, no cotton wedding dress, no
chorus from the *Song of Songs*, no love on the bones, no
tenderness, no escape.

I should remember only love.
One white night I laid awake in your arms,
Watching the moon powder your naked skin.
I cried all night to hold you in my arms
Because this was my dream. I loved you,
I love you.

George & Rue: Pure, Virtuous Killers

They were hanged back-to-back in York County Gaol.

They were rough dreamers, raw believers, set out like killers.

They sprouted in Newport Station, Hants County, Nova Scotia,
in 1925 and 1926.

They smacked a white taxi driver, Silver, with a hammer, to sack his silver.

They bopped Silver and hit backwoods New Brunswick in his black cab.

They slew him in the first hour of January 8, 1949, A.D.

They were clear Negro, and semi-Micmac.

They tooled all night between Fredericton and Saint John with Silver
coiled – a void noose – in the trunk.

They had face-to-face trials in May 1949 and backed each other's guilt.

George Albert Hamilton confessed – to theft – and mated the Sally Anne.

Rufus James Hamilton polished his refined, mint, silver-bright English.

They were dandled from a gallows in the third hour of July 27, 1949, A.D.

They were my cousins, dead a decade before I was born.

My bastard phantasms, my dastard fictions.

Ballad of a Hanged Man

Geo: Their drinks to my drinks feels different.
I'll stomach a stammering teaspoon full,
but Roach laps up half the half bottle.
He slups glass for glass with the best.

I sidled in, easy, the taxi with a hammer,
harsh, in my pocket. See, as a wed man,
I don't care if I wear uglified overalls.
But I ain't gonna hear my child starve.

I had the intention to ruck some money.
In my own heart, I had that, to rape money,
because I was fucked, in my own heart.
I took scared, shaking inside of me.

I knows Fredericton reporters can prove
zoot-suit vines style not my viciousness.
I was shaking all that evening, my mind,
shaking. But my child was hungered.

Have you ever gone in your life, going
two days without eating, and whenever
you get money, you're gonna eat and eat
regardless of all the bastards in Fredericton

was bust in the head, skull jimmied open?
This is what I'm sermonizing in English:
homemade brew, dug up fresh, tastes like
molasses. We had some. Some good.

Logic does not break down these things, sir.
If I hadn't dropped the hammer, laughing,
Silver would be laughing now. Laughing. Silver
moon and snow dropped on the ground.

Two pieces of bone driven two inches
deep in his brain. What's deeper still?
The bones of the skull were bashed
into the brain. Blood railed out.

I was so mixed up, my mind bent crooked.
Silver's neck, face, and hand bleached cold.
Inside the sedan 19-black-49 sobbing Ford.
Outside, snow and ice smelling red-stained.

I ain't dressed this story up. I am enough
disgraced. I swear to the truths I know.
I wanted to uphold my wife and child.
Hang me and I'll not hold them again.

Child Hood I

Geo: Pops beat Ma with belts, branches, bottles.
Anything left-handed. Anything at all.
He'd buck Ma onto the bed, buckle his hips to hers.
Slap her across her breasts, blacken them.

Rue: Her terrorized-and tear-shaped breasts.

He thought her being Mulatto
Was mutilation.

(I miss peanut butter cookies, her sewing machine, the grey gloves
she let me present to a schoolgirl, her preacher-lover-dad's second-
hand Shakespeare and tattered scripture she taught me to read, her
confusingly cream-coloured breasts stupefying dazzling under the
threadbare black disintegrating nightshirt she wore to spoonfeed me
oatmeal.)

Geo: Pops smashed Ma like she was Joe Louis.
Stuck a razor to her throat. Struck her down,
pelted soft flesh with fists and bricks.

Rue: I swung a two-by-four and bust Pop's face open.
Kicked the iron bone that was his skull:
Bleeding was so bad I knelt by the stove like I was praying.
I wanted to be God. I wanted him dead.

Geo: Ma fainted scrubbin some white house's blackened crap-box.
She got a heart stoppage and drooped, *kaput.*

Rue: Years, our only real emotion was hunger.
Our thin bellies had to take rain for bread.

Child Hood II

Rue: I craved blue shoes, a yellow suit, and a green shirt –
and jackets sewn from the torn-off, leather covers of books.
I wanted to don jackets emblazoned with *Eugene Onegin*,
Claudine at School, *Sonnets from the Portuguese*, *The Three Musketeers* –
all the works of Pushkin, Colette, E. B. Browning, and Alexandre Dumas –
all those secretly Negro authors.

Instead, I witnessed all this:

A boy's right arm stuck to a desk with scissors; a father knifed in the gut
while shaking hands with a buddy; two Christians splashed with gasoline
and set ablaze in a church; a harlot garrotted in her bath; a bootlegger
shot through the eye in a liquor store; a banker brained in a vault; two
artists thrown into the Gaspereau River with their hands tied behind
their backs; a pimp machine-gunned to bits outside a school; a divine
getting his throat slit; a poet axed in the back of the neck; a Tory buried
alive in cement; two diabetics fed cyanide secreted in chocolates; a lawyer
decapitated in his office.

Everywhere I saw a Crimea of crime, calamities of houses rigged from
tarpaper and rape, windows blinded with newsprint or burlap sacks. I
could only start the stove with sparks and fear, watch yellow terror eating
yesterday's bad news.

A poor-quality poet crafting hoodlum testimony,
my watery storytelling's cut with the dark rum of curses.

This is how history darkens against its medium.

Hard Nails

Geo: Hard nails split my frail bones;
Hard nails gouge my tomb from stone.
Hard nails pierce my feet and hands,
Tack me down so I can't stand.

Hard nails scratch my frail skin;
Hard nails fasten us chin to chin.
Hard nails I want, hard nails I lack –
Her fingernails ploughin my back.

Drench me down with rum and Coca-Cola.
The gal I kiss be a pretty pretty colour.
I ain't got a dollar, but I ain't got no dolour.
Drench me down with rum and Coca-Cola.

Public Enemy

Rue: Fredericton – fucking – New Brunswick.
A decade of Depression, then the Hitler War.

Carrying my bleak, nasty face out of Nova Scotia,
alarmed, out of Nova Scotia, alarmed,

drift into Fredtown like so much blackstorm sky –
squinting at frigid, ivory, strait-laced streets

speckled by dung of Orange politicians' grins.
(Spy ingots of shit oranging the snow.)

Fredtown was put up by Cadians, Coloureds,
and hammers. Laws and lumber get made here.

Bliss Carman got made here. Why should I put up with
this hard-drinking, hard-whoring, hardscrabble town?

I want to muck up their little white paradise here.
I want to swat their faces til I'm comfortable in my gut.

I want to give em all headaches and nausea:
I'll play *fortissimo* Ellington, blacken icy whiteness.

I'll draw blood the way Picasso draws nudes —
voluptuously.

The Killing

Rue: I ingratiated the grinning hammer
with Silver's not friendless, not unfriendly skull.
Behind him like a piece of storm, I unleashed a frozen glinting –
a lethal gash of lightning.
His soul leaked from him in a Red Sea, a Dead Sea,
churning his clothes to lava.

Geo: No, it didn't look like real blood,
but something more like coal, that inched from his mouth.

Rue: It was a cold hit in the head. A hurt unmassageable.
Car seat left stinking of gas and metal and blood.
And reddening violently.
A rhymeless poetry scrawled his obituary.

Geo: It was comin on us for awhile, this here misery.
We'd all split a beer before iron split Silver's skull.
Silver's muscles still soft and tender. That liquor killed him.
The blood like shadow on his face, his caved-in face.
Smell of his blood over everything.

Rue: Iron smell of the hammer mingled with iron smell of blood
and chrome smell of snow and moonlight.

Geo: He had two hundred dollars on him; bootleg in him.
We had a hammer on us, a spoonful of cold beer in us.

The taxi-driver lies red in the alabaster snow.
His skeleton has taken sick and must be placed in the ground.

This murder is 100 per cent dirt of our hands.

Rue: Twitchy, my hand was twitchy, inside my jacket.
The hammer was gravity: everything else was jumpy.
I wondered if Silver could hear his own blood thundering,
vermilion, in his temples, quickened, twitchy, because of beer;
jumpy molecules infecting his corpuscles, already nervous.

The hammer went in so far that there was no sound –
just the slight mushy squeak of bone.

Silver swooned like the leaden Titanic.
Blood screamed down his *petit-bourgeois* clothes.

Geo: Can we cover up a murder with snow?
With white, frosty roses?

Rue: Here's how I justify my error:
The blow that slew Silver came from two centuries back.
It took that much time and agony to turn a white man's whip
into a black man's hammer.

Geo: No, we needed money,
so you hit the So-and-So,
only much too hard.
Now what?

Rue: So what?

Trial I

Geo: Doc stared gravely, said, "You're going to die."
I glared, spat, "So will you."

. . .

Geo: My speech? Pretty ugly. Those who complain? Uglier.
My English is like fractured China – broken.
I really speak *Coloured*, but with a Three Mile Plains accent.
See, I can't speak Lucasville and my New Road's kinda weak.
Ma English be a desert that don't bloom less watered by rum.

. . .

Geo: Yonder, that horse is fat, its hairs full of sweat.
I love my wife and two childs and I'd hold them yet.

. . .

Geo: This is a good apple country. Right so. I would like to get
on the Dominion Atlantic Railway drivin an engine. If I could go to
Africa, to a Coloured country, or to Haiti, or even to Cuba, I would
go. I would like to get away. On a no-moon night when the only
eyes that got vision are God's. Oh, if I could get away, I would do
away with sickness and not get away with murder. Who can do more
and more and more injustice?

Trial II

Rue: This courtroom's a parliament of jackals –
see Hitler faces front dark robes.

Unsullied, though, a wafer of light silvers water;
unspoiled, the wind rattles alders.

      I would like very much to sing –
in a new life, a new world,
some April song –
"A slight dusting of snow,
the indigo dawn hovers –
and we sweeten in our love,"
yes, something like that,
but blood must expunge, sponge up, blood.

We're condemned because death is not condemned.
We're damned because desire is not damned.

Stars are hanging like locusts in the trees.

Birds faction the air.

April collapses snow into flowers.

The river goes cloudy with moon.

Avowals

A is a cracked steeple.
E is a long scream.
I is a gawky guillotine.
O is a silk abyss.
U is a fetus – or crab lice.
Y is a two-pronged gallows.

Negation

Le nègre negated, meagre, c'est moi:
Denigrated, negative, a local
Caliban, unlikable and disliked
(Slick black bastard—cannibal—sucking back
Licorice-lusty, fifty-proof whisky),
A rusty-pallor provincial, uncouth
Mouth spitting lies, vomit-lyrics, musty,
Masticated scripture. Her Majesty's
Nasty, Nofaskoshan Negro, I mean
To go out shining instead of tarnished,
To take apart *Poetry* like a heart.

So my black face must preface your finish,
Deface your *religion*—unerringly,
Unniggardly, like some *film noir* blackguard's.

Calculated Offensive

à la manière de Baraka

To hell with Pound!
What we desire is African:
Europe is so septic, it seeps poisons.

Why abet the mass murderers
and the famine- and munitions-makers?
All Plato and Aristotle ever did
was waste Nat Turner's time.

Europe?
A machine spewing
fat-assed assassins,
piss-sipping whores,
Chaplinesque Napoleons,
porcine professors analyzing feces!

Who needs all those hymns printed on toilet paper?

Put Europe to the torch:
All of Michelangelo's dripping, syphilitic saints,
all of Sappho's insipid, anorexic virgins.

Use the *Oxford English Dictionary*
and the *Petit Robert* for kindling.

À Dany Laferrière

à la manière de Sade

Think of the Hell-promising virgin—
Swivelled on a hot white stallion, jouncing.
Imagine her lolling in that mount,
A gospel become flesh, a lilting.
Are her eyes burnt-gilty-sapphirish?
Think about that, too.
Are her lips *deux dévergondées*?
Think about that—
And think about her gold hair lashing
Her thighs, milky, honeying.

My pure religion has come to this:
Hushed frigging lust for a yellow-haired
Rouged cut, a naked, cramped space,
My belly jammed on that thin-haired
Mound, succulent, succubine orifice,
Its brown, wiry hairs twined
And twisted into the hairs rooting
My lean bolt plunging and plunging.

Christ, I'd torch a church and sink in Hell
To sink in her just once, that blonde slut,
In Roeg's *Walkabout*, her grey skirt swishing across
Her ass, her white panties winking swank cunt.

Ce trou trempé va être coïté crapuleusement. . . .

Haligonian Market Cry[1]

for Maxine Tynes

I got hallelujah watermelons!—virginal pears!—virtuous corn!
Munit haec et altera vincit!
Luscious, fat-ass watermelons!—plump pears!—big-butt corn!
Le gusta este jardin?
Come-and-get-it cucumbers—hot-to-trot, lust-fresh cucumbers!
Voulez-vous coucher avec moi?
Watermelons!—Go-to-church-and-get-redeemed watermelons!
Un bacio . . . un bacio ancora!
Good God cucumbers!—righteous pears!—golden Baptist corn!
Lieben wir alle nicht die Sinneslust!
I got sluttish watermelons!—sinful cucumbers!—jail-bait
    pears!—
Planted by Big-Mouth Chaucer and picked by Sugar
    Shakespeare!

---

[1] This poem employs Nova Scotia's Latin motto ("One defends and the other
conquers"), a Spanish refrain from Malcolm Lowry's *Under the Volcano* ("Do you
like this garden?"), Italian from Verdi's ("A kiss ... another kiss"), and German
from Berthold Goldschmidt's *Beatrice Cenci* ("All men delight in sensual luxury").

Nu(is)ance

for Wayde Compton

Jabbering double-crossing doubletalk,
Pale-assed poetasters void my "blues-caucused,
Raucous lyrics"—too Negroid and rowdy,
While sable, sassy poets preach I ink
Too blankly, *comme les blancs*, my bleached-out verse
Bleating too whitey-like—worse—in they ears.
What can I say?
        All this blather about
"Black" and "white" verse is blackmail and white noise.
Cripes! English—fallacious—be finished here!
      I'd rather stutter a bastard's language
Only spoken in gutters, a broken,
Vulgar, Creole screech, loud with bawling, slurring,
Balderdash, cussing, and caterwauling,
A corrupt palaver that bankrupts all meeching speech
Because it be literal, guttural *Poetry*,
I.e. *Hubbub*.

Onerous Canon

for Derek Walcott

I

Imbibing libretti and bleak liqueur,
I dread the dim shade of dour, spectral Yeats—

and defrocked, unsavoury Pound, who liked
to put "negros" in lower-case (in their place).

For clarity and charity, I plumb
John Clare, his sugar fire of port and rum.

(But shut away whiny, beseeching Keats,
who should've drunk some *Alexander Keith's*

India Pale Ale!) What can any late
Maker make of literature, painter?

II

O Poet, I suspect you've ogled blues,
golds, greys—adrift in a Venetian sky—

gondola over sodden New Scotland,
and sink in muddy Impressionism—

gilt, scuzzy water in tufted, brown fields,
or gooey ice, drooling with too-soon spring—

what all our reading comes to—a canon
of depression, sorry as January.

Words should vacillate in lascivious postures,
or in notoriously incestuous rhyme. Poet:

One great poem, that's all, but you never fail—
composing lines blustery, yet tender,

your voice your own (Auden in the margins,
Eliot, Yeats, and Pound in the dungeon),

a veriloquous, unadulterated voice,
extracting black blues from a yellowed Oxford.

April 1, 19—

Air smells purely of wine
where I have fallen—
an allegro Negro—

sueing brunette paleness.
Unused to beauty, I
catch the blush of stars,

run my brain along
a line's razor edge,
Basho being sharpest—

or her arrogant thinness!
I draft wrecked words, gulp
draughts of wrecking wine.

To hold her is to hold
perfume—whitest breath
of lilies, or fathom

gold-dark eyes, fierce as Sade.
A brief kiss—one brief kiss—
And I'll breathe the future.

from Blue Elegies

I. i

for David Odhiambo

Blue is a noose strangling the vulnerable sky
Blue is a generic nigger, a genre nigger, an angry nigger
Blue is Della Robbia blue—and fatal, as in Tennessee Williams
Blue is sapphire magenta violet sable diamond dead fur green
Blue is a white body drowned in a glacier and helicoptered to
    a morgue
Blue is a guitar in a Wallace Stevens sonnet carved from *The Cenci*
Blue is *Bombay Sapphire* gin when it's lapped direct from the bottle
Blue is Hitler in bed with Chamberlain in Munich with Eva Braun
Blue is a *saltimbanque* mountebank confusing Scotia Bank
    with a blood bank
Blue is Duke Ellington recording *Indigos* while reading
    Gold Indigoes
Blue is Tory, pot-bellied, smug—just like the *Oxford English
    Dictionary*
Blue is a hole in a bucket that the Atlantic can't fill
Blue is secular, worldly, mundane, global, vulgar, popular,
    plebian, and folksy
Blue is Bessie Smith's murder, still unsolved, though her
    murderer's dead
Blue is John Coltrane—immortal Coltrane—recording *Blue Trane*
Blue is the hippy starved to death by the lucre-hungry yuppy
Blue is ballad recitals by poets praised by *The National Enquirer*
Blue is Jackie O helping out JFK's back by getting on top
Blue is the final Canadian dollar bill
Blue is a field of lavender near Arles, in France, where love is *bleu*
Blue is Bellagio in the rain and Banff in snow squalls
Blue is a Gypsy whose beautiful, tan skin conjures up Three
    Mile Plains, NS
Blue is your worthlessness in the eyes of The Royal Bank
Blue is Chet Baker trying to cop *Blue Moon* after Miles Davis
    has snookered it

Blue is licorice manufactured from liquor and rice
Blue is what happens when you sleep through your moment of
    truth
Blue is snuff films screened in classrooms for literary reasons
Blue is coffee from the Blue Mountains of Jamaica
Blue is a moth huddled in the middle of a sugar bowl as the
    spoon is plunged in
Blue is *Saltwater Spirituals and Deeper Blues; Lush Dreams,*
    Blue Exile; and *Blue*
Fatal, foolhardy poetry.

I. ii

Remember that *shining* going on without you—
near Alexandra School, its fierceness, blasting away
the teacher's scrawl, her numerals, soft, wormy,
squiggling over the blackboard, her majuscules
melting like Hiroshima's eyes, her capitals all shaky
as rickets, the pig-squeal of her white chalk
caught in some, sudden Guernica of sound—
the grating of knives in loud, steel kisses—
because the construction boys next door were pushing
plungers that vomited up mushrooms of dirt and shale,
dynamiting the silence the teachers commended to us
like dictator trainees, but the jackhammers kept
detonating and destroying our ranked grammar,
driving all prim letters into slumping grades.
        Remember this, while, in Cadennabia, absurd, azure waves
packed tighter than a Roman legion on manoeuvres,
explode against the seawall shoreline, darken into green-black,
and leave a vast debris field of gold-brown leaves, fallen,
detonating the image of another grandiose falling
(your black ink sliding rapaciously down the pale page,
your black hand arcing like a dynamiter's gloved mitt)—
the explosive glub-gurgle dissolution
of a sleek Swiss jetliner, off Latinate Nova Scotia
(that is, in pure translation, *New Darkness*),
its glittering beings flaming into the indigo,
all its instant Apollos, shredded into gold debris—
their calendars extinct, their I.D. badges melted down—
three hundred Ovids flung into the void—

I. iii

Everything is holy, as Ginsberg says:
the carpet, the light, the door,
the radio not turned on,
the bedcovers turned back—
like US barbarians at Niagara Falls,
the arteries hardening,
the penis hardening,
the autoeroticism of the pen,
the chair pulled back from the table,
the man pulled away from the woman,
the wastepaper basket clasping an empty *Kleenex* package,
the water bottle announcing I'm thirsty,
the squandered bottle of *Limon Limonero, Liquore di Limone*
(28% alcohol, now only 1/16th of a bottle)—
brackish, sickish, yellow-green in taste, like mustard gas—
the two glasses silenced on the bureau,
the few blue candies—mints—and band-aids under the mirror,
the lamp on, on the table,
the watch eyeing 4h,
the white and purple flowers dying, drooping halfway out
    of their round, glassed grave/womb of water,
the black ink pacified in the bottle,
the history of Mussolini's assassination calm in its prose,
or orderly as bullets,
the firing squad so fiery in the blood,
the depleted film canister, black and brooding,
the finished manuscripts and the unfinished books,
all discoursing together—
Ovid's *Poetry of Exile* abutting on Massey's opera on English,
French, and Yiddish lovers in Québec—
the mirror giving back the wall,
The President's Daughter lying suggestively under *The Paradox
    of Cruelty,*
the pencil looking pensive

(bee-coloured, yellow and black, like a scrawny mulatto),
the MCI *Calling Card* advertising pricey repartee,
the terracotta-looking floor tiles,
the comfortable Italian sandals looking comfortable with the tiles
(like two races, miscegenated),
the curtains drawn (but not "haggard" or "quartered"),
the woman next door probably asleep and alone,
the telephone condemned,
Le Lucciole sixty-nining *Le Ore Super*
(two women's four eyes purring languor),
the insolence and sorrow of now 4h,
these words saying too much,
these words condemning the poem,
the breath drawing sharp as guillotines,
the hand quivering,
the idea of reading Fowlie on Rimbaud,
the idea of reading folly,
the dead small bottle of *Schweppes* ("Since 1783") *Limone* on
      the floor,
the racy postcards raring to go,
the Italian travel brochure abridging Canada
(*Self Drive Package: Canada in Libertà*:
scarlet, with a white border, and the half-tone
of a gigantic maple leaf dominating the cover),
the two black pens lying, faggish, together—
the fountain pen and the *Bic* ballpoint pen—
the pen always lying,
the brassy coins stacked shaky as the Tower of Pisa—
amounting to four L.1000 and three L.200 coins—
the *Autobiography of William Butler Yeats*
conspiring with *The Memoirs of Frederic Mistral*
(both Nobel laureates, one unread),
the memory of JFK in the Villa Serbelloni,
the memory of Pliny the Younger in marble,
the empty, brown, hand-made, Québécois shoes under the desk,
the memory of the ferry yesterday to Cannenabia
(and that spelling is wrong),

Tremezzo in the distance,
the baroquely glowing water,
the men with long fishing rods,
the carping, Freudian imagery,
the words *Allegata copia omaggio* imposed on the *fausse*
     blonde's forehead,
the depressed light switch,
the switch from *vers blanc* to *vers libre*,
the black camera in its blacker case,
the *camera obscura* that is the brain,
the bicameral Parliament lost across the Atlantic,
the chiaroscuro of sunlight over Bellagio,
the collapse of Pescalo into its cool, piss-scent alleys,
the blonde tourist inviting,
the others scowling,
the memory of the lone black woman youngish in a rose coat,
bella, under an umbrella by the ferry terminal in Bellagio,
the drizzle of leaves,
the arm-pits itchy with deodorant,
the memory of the *bancomat* and the Sao Paolo bank in
     Cadennabia (?),
the closed closet door with the brass handle,
the shadow of the half-turned key,
the scrolling of liquid (probably water) in my stomach,
the pitiless Italian porno photographed at f:64
so that each pubic hair is viciously vivid,
the utterance's pleasurable closure,
the immaculate ejaculation.

I. iv

for Djanet Sears

After the black-and-brown-faced oasis
Of Chateau-Rouge, its leather and Saturday aphrodisiacs—
The slap of fish against the tang of the *Koran*,
The white folks *et leurs flics* miraculously scarce—
I navigate Montmartre, slurp Marzadro's *Liquore*
All'Uovo Grand Uovo, an egg liqueur,
Some 17% alcohol, and request a *cambio*.
So, a stunned clerk asks, "Do you speak Spanish?"
I answer, "Canadian," and she laughs and laughs.

And it's raining sprinkles, drizzling like a Nazi smile,
Here at Square de Mont-Cenis,
A withered, fickle nun spying on me from her window,
The rain speckling, then heckling, the stones,
My left foot hating the hard edges of the cobblestones,
Until I escape into Sacré-Coeur,
A fountain of white marble and gold-silver light,
Where Christ, Hollywood-holy in ivory and gold leaf,
His Gallic face bleached of passion,
Peers through ruddy, stained-glass windows
That bleed like assassinated, executed Africa.

A provincial and a heathen, I worship
The Montmartre of the African Baptist Church,
Its white-washed pinewood, not white marble,
Its saints imagined out of unlettered ministers,
Its *arpents de neige*, not cobblestoned alleys,
Its ducking ponds, not the Octobrishly burnt umber Seine,
Its fearsome scarecrows, not ghoulish crucifixes,
And then the Chateau-Rouge of Halifax—
Lebanese-Vietnamese-Africadian Gotti'gen Street,
Its terrors and treasures, the black girls
Sitting on the low wall girdling the Library,
Or in the meat market in the Derby Tavern,
While a salt-spray mullah cries, "Maaackerel, fresh
Maaackerel!", and scripture distills rum.

I. v

October, Gothic October: no lovers loiter, lounge,
in Annapolis Royal's "Historic Gardens."
Naturally: Love poems wither in our bleak, stony,
frigid, hostile, brutal Canuck anthologies.
Maybe all hardy Canadian poetry erupts lavishly
from some solitary, sullen naturalist's notebook.
See! A last bee, still stockpiling pollen, hums hotly
against this Octobral creep of cold. Octopoid
networks and wires of downed branches and briars
and twigs, prickling and muddling and needling, obscure
a scrappy bit of light, famished, gorging on a slice
of brown-black, brackish, leaf-plastered,
subsidiary pond, wafting orange-green-brown lily pads
and a certain tangy tart stink—
maybe of algae and oak leaves, decaying,
and the *bizz* of wispy, final, waifish insects.
Everything here is allegory for allegations.
Look! The dyked marsh is sucking, slurping, the Fundy—
the tall, hay-like grass, hay-smelling, springs
out of rank black mud, crabby, with fronds and fringes of muck,
then sodden, mud-coralled water giving back
a sky of grey-and-white-peppered clouds, blue shards also,
conjoining dark evergreen spikes,
grey, ghostly, scrawny things, or gold or gold-orange sprays
and tufts the colour of a blonde *fillette*.
Nearby accumulates a pungent cascade of leaves,
then the thick, gigantic stalks of marsh grass,
with sunlight baying in—nostalgic, regretful, imploring—
like the speaker in a John Thompson *ghazal*,
with the last maniacal mosquitoes, whining, *comme des pleûtres*,
and strafing still-fragrant, still-bloody roses,
near where the train tracks are *Kaput*, all torn up now,
these roses glistening and perfuming dogmatically
while the eye hooks on notorious, flagrant, orange-red trees

and bowers of vines, other overhanging things,
darkening, just as the sun darkens while first launching light
against the dykes, the marsh, in dying brilliance
equivalent to what Carman paints in "Low Tide at Grand Pré."
Dismissive of our idiot anxieties and ironies,
stately lances the august, sepulchral, elegiac light.

I. vi
for George Boyd

Rain-scruffed yellow-stone,
weather-wrinkled as bark,
    is like bark, flood-lit by rain;
and the harbour is slate,
    heaving like a black lung—
or a cascade of rats' paws
    tearing at the boats barged
against chafing wharves,
    those tongues cunnilingusing
the salt-blistered waves.
    The wind stinks of pitch or oil;
boats wobble back and forth
    like Liberal Party rhetoric,
the keel and rudder uncertain,
    while the *Imperoyal* Refinery's
hellish, deathless flame smudges
    the night-bitter air, its broth
and chowder of pollution.
    If only snow or rain cascading
through smoky, cranky alleys,
    could tint this city of raw war
petrifyingly beautiful! But its
    history sanctifies sanguinary horror:
the legislature's flanked by Howe,
    defiant, and a Boer War soldier,
La Liberté guidant le peuple.
    So orange light goes up as prayer
and comes down leaf-dark,
    rotten as crushed cockroaches,
and pornographic drizzle
    lays dirty rain and explicit sleet:
this *King Lear* weather heaps up
    snow and shotgunned corpses.

Winter-closed roses look vase-
    shaped; the harbour is stone
leeching black water, leaking
    black water, near the winged
lion that Venice gave Halifax,
    the Workers' Sodom, the Vatican
of *Vice*, where every clock
    suffers cardiac arrest at 9:06 a.m.,
December 6, 1917,
    when eyes spiked on glass,
and molten iron rained on the streets
    and War paraded home viciously,
and all the light was smoke.

Blues de Malcolm

If you're down and out,
Good and Evil don't matter.
If you're down, dirty and out,
Vice and Virtue don't matter.
But if you're up and coming,
Your innocence will shatter.

Now I go from drink to drink
And I've gone from gal to gal.
Yes, I slip from bad to worse,
And I've fallen from gal to gal:
The ones I want promise Paradise,
The ones I get give me hell.

I ain't blue: the rain still works;
The wind hasn't broken down.
I ain't blue: the rain, it still works,
The wind ain't all fallen down.
And the sun, it still burns, it burns,
It burns right down to the ground.

May ushers in with lilac

May ushers in with lilac—
sweet apple blossoms too—
cutting in buttery,
fluttering,
suave colours of cream plum
and honey *pluviôse*
plus perfumes fuming
musky lemon,
and smells of cedar in fresh rain.

We are not only
    philosophies and religions,
languages and 'races,'
    but also skin and teeth
thought and blood
    and on that basis,
that axis
    yes, *oui*, may amalgamate
and mate and propogate
    just as we wish.

Our children will be
    every colour eyes can know,
and free:
    and states, parents, gods,
must have no say:
    Love is a tyrannical democracy.

Vive le Québec
Vive le Québec
Vive le Québec libéré.

Vive aussi le Québec de couleur-
Toutes les couleurs.
Vivre notre québécité.

George & Rue: Coda

Near midnight, Rufus slammed the hammer
Down, down —bam! — into Burgundy's head —

Like a bullet bashing the skull.
The night heard a man halloo, "Oh!"

At that stabbing noise, George whipped around.
The hurt cab bled as black as a hearse.

The moon that night: a white man's face.
Winds flickered black, slick, in the pines.

When Georgie sidled down the hill, glidin
Back to the car, Br'er Rudy already had

Burgundy's wallet tugged out his pocket.
Blood hugged Rue's body, snuggled up

His face. Giorgio shoved Burgundy aside,
So he could fist cash, watch, rosary, coins.

Later, George stove the taxi, a cadaver
Fluffed in the trunk, in Fredericton's snow,

And slinked off, whistling, to drink, drink, drink.
Snow cleansed everything, but memory.

The taxicab leaked a smoke-trail of blood.
Just because.

Georgie weren't chilled; he waltzed back where
Rue be guzzlin blackberry wine in brand-new clothes.

Rue ain't feel nothin bad or wrong or upset.
A white man was dead, yes; but they had booze and cash.

Letter to a Young Poet

Go ahead and compose a poem on *Love*:
You'll poison it with the poetry —
Sly darkness without any sweetness.
See, the poet's body whelps carrion-insects,
Vomits some worms, some ants, some wasps, some bees —
Things malevolent and marvellous at once,
Their horrifically mixed-up mouths chewing,
Ripping, devastating, your heart.
Poetry eats its lovers alive.
        You could get your throat slashed for this —
This ominous obsession.
                But you have no shame:
No, you have the face of a crushed horse,
And capering therein a million maggots
Usurping every prickle of light.

Of Black English, or Pig Iron Latin

for Kaie Kellough

My brain were brass, fucked, alloyed
By alliteration. It were dazzlingly dull
For a nigger, niggling with English,
Haggling o'er some moping poem,
Cut from a second-hand grammar,
Rhyming Oxonian *et* Negronian.
       Zounds! My lyrics was tin-plate,
Not steel-sheet, some gift of gabble,
Une blague, maybe glib bilge.
Oui? What was needed were, was —
After some hectic loss of respect —
Higher quality coal — or iron — or gold ...

(A tinny Walcott, I would like, I'd like,
Black English to sound more like tempered steel.)

Africadian Experience
(For Frederick Ward)

To howl in the night because of smoked rum wounding the heart;
To be so stubbornly crooked, your alphabet develops rickets;
To check into the Sally Ann — and come out brain-dead, but spiffy;
To smell the sewer anger of politicians washed up by dirty votes;
To feel your skin burning under vampire kisses meant for someone else;
To trash the ballyhooed verses of the original, A-1, Africville poets;
To carry the Atlantic into Montreal in epic suitcases with Harlem accents;
To segregate black and white bones at the behest of discriminating worms;
To mix voodoo alcohol and explosive loneliness in unsafe bars;
To case the Louvre with raw, North Preston gluttony in your eyes;
To let vitamin deficiencies cripple beauty queens in their beds;
To dream of Halifax and its collapsing houses of 1917
       (Blizzard and fire in ten thousand living rooms in one day);
To stagger a dirt road that leads to an exploded piano and bad sermons;
To plumb a well that taps rice wine springing up from China;
To okay the miracle of a split length of wood supporting a clothesline;
To cakewalk into prison as if you were parading into Heaven;
To recognize *Beauty* when you see it and to not be afraid.

Afterword

Let Us Now Attain Polyphonous Epiphanies

On a sunny Saturday Halifax, Nova Scotia, afternoon in April 1972, my father gathered up his three sons and a few of our friends, crowded us all into a station wagon, and just went driving. I sat up front, near the car radio, and listened intently as Bobby Vinton sang "Sealed with a Kiss" (from sometime back in the 1950s), but I also concentrated on the hits of the day, such as those by the Jackson 5 ("ABC") and by the Osmonds ("One Bad Apple"). This attentiveness was memorably strange, for I knew it was separating me irrevocably from my childhood. Indeed, one chum riding with us was a girl I had a crush on, and the radio songs were suddenly communicating my inarticulate angst and exposing my secret desire. Later that day, I borrowed the portable radio, laid down in my bed, in my room, and tuned the set to the Top 40 songs that had just begun to speak to—and for—me. I laid there with my eyes closed, fantasizing about that girl, while letting song after song alert me to the promise of the kiss, the embrace, the dance, and even everlasting love.

I think I became a poet then, though I did not begin to write what I called "songs" for another three years. I became a songwriter—a lyricist—before I became, indelibly, a poet, so I learned to state my yearnings and my fears in a heart-felt, three-minute formula—a sincere *orature*, straight from the gut, and straight to an auditing girl's ear. (Some of us young "bloods" loved to sing, late night, strategically, beneath the windows of neighbours' daughters.)

It was to become a better songsmith that I began to write poetry, at age sixteen, in 1976, after reading Ezra Pound's translation of Li Po's "Song of Chang-Kan," which Pound rebrands as "The River-Merchant's Wife: A Letter." (The millennium-old Chinese poem struck my teen ears as Mississippi blues.) Then, to be a better poet, I began to ransack every bit of poetry in the Halifax North End Memorial Library, which had opened early in 1968 and whose name remembered the victims of the Halifax Explosion of December 6, 1917.

But that library was special for another reason: it was set in the downtown centre of immigrant, working-class, military, and Afrocentric Halifax: the fabled North End and its wrecked British (Cockney version) accents, its vocabulary of rum-soaked, extra-salty Billingsgate, and its deep immersion in both naval brass bands and street corner, rhythm and blues balladry. Hence, the poetry I picked off the library shelves didn't consist only of translated Dante and the greatest hits of Ramblin' Billy Shakespeare but also wanton tons of Afro-Americana, "Negro" verse, come all the way from Harlem, Chi-Town, and L.A.

I read intensively the glow-in-the-dark names: Langston Hughes, LeRoi Jones (Amiri Baraka), Gwendolyn Brooks, Alice Walker, and Ishmael Reed. But I most adored the sultry, smoky verse of Jean Toomer (see *Cane*), the Southern-fried songs of Sterling Brown, the soul anthems of Carolyn M. Rodgers, the mystical bohemianism of Conrad Kent Rivers, the intellectual dandyism of Melvin B. Tolson, the Africanist musings of Henry Dumas, and, above all, the beautiful, baroque decors, gutbucket music, and history-informed genius of Robert Hayden (1913–1980), a pupil of W.H. Auden—and the blues.

True: most of the names in the previous paragraph will be mysteries to most English Canadian poets and readers. But my strengths as a poet, whatever they are, derive from the sonic universe of African American verse *and* song. I am proud that my early influences were not just the dour nationalists, strenuous environmentalists, and funky feminists of English Canadian canonical legend but also—and adamantly *more*—the multicultural sense of Hayden, the cosmopolitanism of Rivers and Tolson, the earthy roots appeal of Toomer, Brown, and Dumas, and the Aretha Franklin–like realism of Rodgers.

Oui, j'ai lu les "Canucks": My "ado" faves were Leonard Cohen (Mr. *Superstar*), A.M. Klein, Irving Layton, Gwendolyn MacEwen, Alden Nowlan, and Raymond Souster. But though I admired these poets, and idolized Layton, I am more a product of *The Revolutionary Young Black Poets* than I am of *The Penguin Book of Canadian Verse*.

Thus, in Queen Elizabeth High School (named for a Monarch no one ever thought of, except during Royal Visits and Royal Scandals), I inked poems that were African American in intent but also pop-music-influenced. I bought Bruce Springsteen's album *Born to Run* in 1975, but my brother, Bryant, brought home Parliament's transformative *Chocolate City* in 1976. Then I found romance, a breakup, and Bob Dylan's written vocals. Of his oeuvre, I turntabled again and again those 1960s classics—*Another Side of Bob Dylan*, *Bringing It All Back Home*, *Highway 61 Revisited*, *Blonde on Blonde*, and *John Wesley Harding*—and, two from the 1970s, *Blood on the Tracks* and *The Basement Tapes*. (Ironically, I discovered Af-Am—"FM"—blues music through Dylan, one of its most studious devotees.) To reformulate T.S. Eliot's self-identification, I was, as a tyro bard, Poundian in poetics, Dylanesque in politics, and African American in faith.

Between high school graduation in 1978 and jetting to the University of Waterloo in 1979, I spent a year trying to organize a Black Youth Organization, an effort that spawned several provincial conferences and, most importantly, saw me visit, for the first time in my life, most of Nova Scotia's several dozen African American—established or (in Cape Breton) West Indian–founded communities. I could not help but notice the rural loveliness of these villages and the extravagant beauty of their nymphs. The locale that seemed most romantic was Weymouth Falls, in Digby County, settled in 1783 by African American Loyalists. There I met one special family and one jewel of a woman. I began to associate her with the Sissiboo River, Mount Beulah and its African Baptist Church, and even the sawmill and the dam, not to mention country songs, smelts fried in vinegar, and hotcombs, and a husky voice.

Casing English in southwestern Upper Canada in 1979, I experienced two shifts in my life: (1) Unexpected homesickness drove me to learn all I could about Nova Scotia, the Maritimes, and, specifically, my own people, the lost Black Atlantic tribe of "Scotians"; (2) I underwent a thorough indoctrination in the British poetic canon. Thus, I emerged with an Honours B.A. that represented a serious, autodidact knowledge of Black Nova Scotia and a studious *vers blanc* poetic gleaned from *three* readings of Jack Milton's *Paradise Lost*, canvassing of the Romantics (Willy Blake and Billy Wordsworth), strenuous encounters with "Shaky," and even Frygian tutelage on the Bible (Hebrew and Greek). I also memorized pieces of Gerard Manley Hopkins and Dylan Thomas.

When my first book, *Saltwater Spirituals and Deeper Blues*, appeared in 1983, it applied, more or less, Milton and Hopkins to Nova Scotian African Baptist church history. But it also included "Watercolour for Negro Expatriates in France," a strongly African American–oriented poem I wrote as New Year's Eve 1978 became New Year's Day 1979. This poem was the first that told me I could honourably title myself a poet. (Because it criticizes African American artists, it is also, though I didn't know it then, an explicitly African Canadian lyric.)

Homing to Nova Scotia in 1985 (after a year of newspaper editorship in Waterloo, Ont.), I found employment with the Black United Front (a provincially funded, black-oriented social agency) as a social worker in the Annapolis Valley. Now back in Weymouth Falls and back again in "love" (several times over—simultaneously), I also, suddenly, heard all those countrified, Negro voices as Miltonic, Shakespearean, bluesy, epic, classical, and, simply, lyrical.

In graduate school at Dalhousie University, in the fall of 1986, I took Prof. John Fraser's great course, "Tradition and Experimentation in Modern Poetry,

1880–1920." I read passionately—again—Pound, Eliot, Blake, Thomas, and Hopkins, but also Arthur Rimbaud, Charles Baudelaire, W.B. Yeats, and William Carlos Williams, and added Ovid, Catullus, Jules Laforgue, Alexander Pushkin, John Clare, and Federico García Lorca. In a CanLit class, I finally read George Bowering, John Thompson, and Michael Ondaatje (the hero of my M.A. thesis). Then, browsing the journal *Callaloo*, I found Afro-America's diva, Rita Dove, and the soon-to-be Caribbean Nobel laureate-in-poetry Derek Walcott.

While yet a M.A. student, I published a North End Halifax newspaper, *The Rap*, which boasted, of its eight pages, one ad-free sheet dedicated, naturally, to poetry. Though only a slim, monthly tabloid, with a miniscule circulation of 7,000, *The Rap* broke several stories that won national notice, including that of Dr. Howard McCurdy, Ph.D., and MP for Windsor-Walkerville. Hired in 1987 to be his constituency liaison, I began to type up poetry in the House of Commons.

My first narrative lyric suite, *Whylah Falls* (1990), was born of this matrix of journalism, pop song, social activism, parliamentary *bavardage*, and "degreed" poesy. It is in its pages that my poetics, which I term, *ahem*, "Revelationism," receives its first conscious exposition. Its tenets are rudimentary: "Form is as form does"; "Make it beautiful"; "The secret is to sing": *Everything can be poetry.*

(I'll add that, for me, the Projectivist project of "composition by field" means *constructing* the *whole* book *qua* book, not just each poem or page. Hence, in my books, I tend to include an epigraph about *Beauty*, photographs, a blues poem, and at least one juvenile lyric.)

I wish I could claim to expound some grandiose theory, such as the L=A=N=G=U=A=G=E idiom or the "Ecopoetics" approach. But, golly, when all's said and done, I remain, fundamentally, a songwriter.

Fittingly then, my successor to *Whylah Falls* was *Beatrice Chancy*, published as an opera libretto in 1998 and as a verse-play in 1999, and staged as an opera in 1998, 1999, and 2001. (Begun during my doctoral studies at Queen's University [1990–93], *Beatrice Chancy* fuses Romanticism— Shelley's—with the sassiness of Sade, the Gothic flavour of the slave narratives, and the ghetto veracity of Wanda Coleman.) Two other opera libretti and verse-plays have followed: *Québécité* in 2003 and *Trudeau: Long March / Shining Path* in 2007. Yet, I still jet lyrics, as represented by *Gold Indigoes* (2000), *Blue* (2001), and *Black* (2006), and pen narrative lyric suites, as represented by *Execution Poems* (2000) and *Illuminated Verses* (2005).

Distantly tracing Walcott, I want to cap my art with an epic, one I began recently (in Zanzibar), with the working title of *Hymns: Canticles of the*

Colored Baptists of Nova Scotia. It marks a return to my roots—in subject (a meditation on the African diaspora to the Americas), but also style—the use of a collage of verse forms to structure a narrative. The catalyst is Walcott, the model is Pound, and the result, should I succeed, will be a type of *Bible*.

To move toward a conclusion, lemme admit I be a Negro rhetorician, orator, actor, and *singer*. Yep, hear my loud, raucous, *Africadian* voice. Ain't no shame in that, folks. Yep. I's a *bel canto* cannibal (Caliban), pickin over the livin body and booty of the Anglo-Saxon, literary imperium to do what my forebears did: (try to) make it newfangled *and* pretty. (And if I be a street preacher, an opera singer, what, pray tell, is ma crime?) I feel a kinship with the *paroxysme* that Ira Nadel terms the "violent, explosive lyricism associated with the Symbolists ..."[1] Then again, the only poet I've ever dreamt of is Pound,[2] a fact which I think relates to Jonathan Gill's assertion that "Pound clearly recognized the affinities between his own use of Provençal song forms and [Langston] Hughes' use of the blues— in both cases, a vernacular, 'closed' form was being used to produce a surprising vitality and freshness."[3] I's tries to do sumpin similar,[4] believing, along with Michael Alexander, that "Beauty ... has fallen on hard times and ought to be rescued."[5]

So call me a "maximalist,"[6] or say I scribe "vernacular formalism":[7] I don't care—so long as I be sounded, recited, sung.

—*George Elliott Clarke*

Notes

1 Nadel, ed., *The Letters of Ezra Pound to Alice Corbin Henderson* (Austin, TX: University of Texas Press, 1993), 144n17.
2 In Spring 1985.
3 Gill, "Ezra Pound and Langston Hughes: The ABC of Po'try," in *Ezra Pound and African American Modernism*, ed. Michael Coyle (Orono, ME: National Poetry Foundation, 2001), 84.
4 The supreme bards? James Brown b/w Syl Cheney-Coker.
5 Alexander, *The Poetic Achievement of Ezra Pound* (Edinburgh: University of Edinburgh Press, 1998), 100.
6 M. Travis Lane, "Maximalist Poetry," *The Fiddlehead* 172 (Summer 1992): 141.
7 Kevin McNeilly, "Word Jazz 2," *Canadian Literature* 165 (Summer 2000): 181.

Acknowledgements

From *Lush Dreams, Blue Exile: Fugitive Poems*
Pottersfield Press, Lawrencetown Beach, N.S., 1994
  Salvation Army Blues
  Halifax Blues
  Hammonds Plains African Baptist Church
  Campbell Road Church
  Watercolour for Negro Expatriates in France

From *Whylah Falls*, 2nd ed.
Polestar Press, Vancouver, 2000
  Look Homeward, Exile
  The Wisdom of Shelley
  The River Pilgrim: A Letter
  Blank Sonnet
  The Symposium
  Rose Vinegar
  Blues for X
  Vision of Justice

From *Beatrice Chancy*
Polestar Book Publishers, Victoria, 1999
  Chancy's Menu
  Chancy's Drinking Song
  Beatrice's Defence

From *Execution Poems: The Black Acadian Tragedy of "George and Rue"*
Gaspereau Press, Wolfville, N.S., 2001
  George & Rue: Pure, Virtuous Killers
  Ballad of a Hanged Man
  Child Hood I
  Child Hood II
  Hard Nails

Public Enemy
The Killing
Trial I
Trial II
Avowals

From *Blue*
Raincoast Books, Vancouver, 2001
Negation
Calculated Offensive
À Dany Laferrière
Haligonian Market Cry
Nu(is)ance
Onerous Canon
April 1, 19–
I.i, I.ii, I.iii, I.iv, I.v, I.vi, from *Blue Elegies*

From *Québécité: A Jazz Fantasia in Three Cantos*
Gaspereau Press, Kentville, N.S., 2003
Blues de Malcolm
May ushers in with lilac

From *Black*
Raincoast Books, Vancouver, 2006
George & Rue: Coda
Letter to a Young Poet
Of Black English or Pig Iron Latin
Africadian Experience